TO: _____

FROM: _____

Come to me, all you who are weary and burdened,

and I will give you rest.

—Matthew 11:28

## ZondervanPublishingHouse

Mail Drop B20
Grand Rapids, Michigan 49530
http://www.zondervan.com

**Editorial Director:** Joy Marple
**Project Editor:** Robin Schmitt
**Production Editor:** Pat Matuszak
**Art Director:** Robin Welsh
**Designer:** Christopher Tobias/Tobias Design
**Photographer:** William J. Hebert

Printed in China
97 98 99 /HK/ 3 2 1

# FINDING

*peace*

*Photography by William J. Hebert*

ZondervanGifts
*We have a gift for inspiration™*

The Lord is to be our source of supply. In him are springs, fountains, and streams that will never be cut off or run dry. **To those who are anxious comes the gracious promise of our heavenly Father:** If he is the source of our mercies, mercy will never fail us.

IN THE WILDERNESS SHALL WATERS BREAK OUT,
AND STREAMS IN THE DESERT.

—Isaiah 35:6 KJV

My peace I give you. —John 14:27

Two painters were once asked to paint a picture illustrating their own ideas of rest. *The first chose for his scene a quiet, lonely lake, nestled among mountains far away.* The second, using swift, broad strokes on his canvas, painted a thundering waterfall. Beneath the falls grew a fragile birch tree, bending over the foam. *On its branches, nearly wet with the spray from the falls, sat a robin on its nest.* The first painting was simply a picture of stagnation and inactivity. *The second, however, depicted rest.*

—Drummond

THE PEACE OF GOD, WHICH TRANSCENDS

ALL UNDERSTANDING, WILL GUARD YOUR HEARTS

AND YOUR MINDS IN CHRIST JESUS.

—Philippians 4:7

When God is the center of a soul, although disasters may crowd in on all sides and roar like the waves of the sea, there is a constant calm within. The world can neither give nor take away this kind of peace.

— Archbishop Leighton

God gives quietness in the midst of the raging storm.... *He waves his hand, signaling the end of the raging tempest and the beginning of the restful calm.* His voice is heard above the screaming of the wind through the ropes and rigging, and over the thrashing of the waves. *"Quiet! Be still!"* (Mark 4:39). Can you not hear it? *And instantly there is a great calm.*

God giveth quietness. —Job 34:29 KJV

SURELY I AM WITH YOU ALWAYS.

—Matthew 28:20

Do not look ahead to what may happen tomorrow. The same everlasting Father who cares for you today will take care of you tomorrow and every day. Either he will shield you from suffering or he will give you his unwavering strength that you may bear it. Be at peace, then, and set aside all anxious thoughts and worries.

—Frances de Sales

Let him who walks in the dark, who has no light,

trust in the name of the LORD. —Isaiah 50:10

Only the peace of God will quiet our minds and put our hearts at rest. *We must place our hand in his as a little child and allow him to lead us into the bright sunshine of his love.* He knows the way out of the dense, dark forest, so may we climb into his arms, trusting him to rescue us by showing us the shortest and most reliable road.

—Dr. Pardington

One of the blessings of the old-time Sabbath day was the calmness, restfulness, and holy peace that came from having a time of quiet solitude away from the world. There is a special strength that is born in solitude. Crows travel in flocks, and wolves in packs, but the lion and the eagle are usually found alone.

JESUS WENT UP ON A MOUNTAINSIDE BY HIMSELF.

—Matthew 14:23

Be still, and know that I am God. —Psalm 46:10

Place the storm of your individual troubles on God's altar of everyday trials, and the same night, the Lord will appear to you. *His rainbow will extend across the subsiding flood, and in your stillness you will hear the everlasting music.*

—George Matheson

MAY GOD HIMSELF, THE GOD OF PEACE,

SANCTIFY YOU THROUGH AND THROUGH.

—1 Thessalonians 5:23

Holiness makes the soul like a field or garden of God, with every kind

of pleasant fruit and flower, and each one delightful and undisturbed,

enjoying a sweet calm and the gentle and refreshing rays of the sun.

—Jonathan Edwards

Dew will never appear while there is either heat or wind.

*The temperature must fall, the wind cease, and the air come to a point of coolness and rest—absolute rest—before the invisible particles of moisture will become dew to dampen any plant or flower.* And the grace of God does not come forth to bring rest and renewal to our soul until we completely reach the point of stillness before him.

This is the resting place, let the weary rest. —Isaiah 28:12

GOD'S COMMAND, "DO NOT BE ANXIOUS ABOUT ANYTHING"
(PHILIPPIANS 4:6), IS UNLIMITED, AND SO IS THE VERSE,
"CAST ALL YOUR ANXIETY ON HIM" (1 PETER 5:7).

—Dr. Payson

What I really needed was the deep ocean of God's love, and the high mountains of his truth within me. His wisdom had depths and heights that neither the ocean nor the mountains could contain and that could not be compared with jewels, gold, or precious stones.

—Margaret Bottome

Lᴏʀᴅ, you have been our dwelling place

throughout all generations. —Psalm 90:1

God is your Father. *Can you state that truth with full*

*assurance and faith?* Once you do, your dove of faith will no

longer wander the skies in restless flight but will settle

forever in its eternal resting place of peace: your Father!

—Arthur Christopher Bacon

Dear Father, I am coming to meet with you. Nothing on the common, everyday plain of life will keep me away from your holy heights. At your calling I come, so I have the assurance that you will meet with me. Each morning begun so well on the mountain will make me strong and glad the rest of the day!

—Joseph Parker

GOD IS OUR REFUGE AND STRENGTH,

AN EVER-PRESENT HELP IN TROUBLE.

—Psalm 46:1

Isaac went out to the field one evening to meditate. —Genesis 24:63

People living in cities today would do well to follow the example of Isaac and as often as possible visit the fields of the countryside, away from the hustle and bustle of the city…. *A walk through a field, a stroll by a seashore, or a hike across a meadow sprinkled with daisies will purge you of the impurities of life and will cause your heart to beat with new joy and hope.*

WHERE MORNING DAWNS AND EVENING FADES
YOU CALL FORTH SONGS OF JOY.

—Psalm 65:8

Have you ever risen early, climbed a hill, and watched God make a morning? The dull gray gives way as he pushes the sun toward the horizon, and then the tints and hues of every color begin to blend into one perfect light as the full sun suddenly bursts into view. As king of the day, the sun moves majestically across the sky, flooding the earth and every deep valley with glorious light. At this point, you can hear the music of heaven's choir as it sings of the majesty of God himself and of the glory of the morning.

Being restless and having worries and cares are absolutely forbidden by our Lord, who said, "So do not worry, saying, 'What shall we eat?' or 'What shall we drink?' or 'What shall we wear?'" (Matthew 6:31). *He does not mean that we are not to think ahead or that our life should never have a plan or pattern to it. He simply means that we are not to worry about these things.*

—the Rev. Darlow Sargeant

May your unfailing love rest upon us, O LORD,

even as we put our hope in you. —Psalm 33:22

MY PEACE I GIVE WHEN PRAYER SEEMS LOST, UNHEARD;

KNOW MY PROMISES ARE EVER IN MY WORD.

All the peace, happiness, and power of the Christian life hinges on one thing. That one thing is taking God at his Word, believing he really means exactly what he says.

—Frances Ridley Havergal

The LORD longs to be gracious to you;

The greenest grass is found wherever the most rain falls. So I suppose it is the fog and mist of Ireland that makes it "the Emerald Isle." *And wherever you find the widespread fog of trouble and the mist of sorrow, you always find emerald green hearts that are full of the beautiful foliage of the comfort and love of God.*

—Charles H. Spurgeon

There is nothing that makes the Scriptures more precious to us than a time of "captivity." The old psalms of God's Word have sung for us with compassion by our stream at Babel and have resounded with new joy as we have seen the Lord deliver us from captivity and "restore our fortunes, … like streams in the Negev" (Psalm 126:4).

—William Taylor

*peace*

ALL MY SPRINGS OF JOY ARE IN YOU.

—Psalm 87:7  NASB

his my song through endless ages,

Jesus led me all the way.

The shepherds of the Alps have a beautiful custom of ending the day by singing an evening farewell to one another. *The air is so pure that the songs can be heard for very long distances.* As the sun begins to set, they gather their flocks and begin to lead them down the mountain paths while they sing, *"'Thus far has the LORD helped us.'"*(1 Samuel 7:12) Let us praise his name!

"Come, come," he calls you, "O soul oppressed and weary,
Come to the shadows of my desert rest;
Come walk with me far from life's noisy discords,
And peace will breathe like music in your breast."

Be all at rest, so then you'll be an answer

To those who question, "Who is God and where?"

For God is rest, and where he dwells is stillness,

And they who dwell in him, his rest will share.

And what will meet the deep unrest around you,

But the calm peace of God that filled his breast?

For still a living voice calls to the weary,

From him who said, "Come unto me and rest."

—Freda Hanbury Allen

Though the fig tree does not bud and there are no grapes on the vines, *though the olive crop fails and the fields produce no food,* though there are no sheep in the pen and no cattle in the stalls, *yet I will rejoice in the* LORD, *I will be joyful in God my Savior.*

—Habakkuk 3:17–18

Don't you know that day dawns after night, showers displace drought, and spring and summer follow winter? Then, have hope! Hope forever, for God will not fail you! —Charles H. Spurgeon

THE LORD GIVES STRENGTH TO HIS PEOPLE;

THE LORD BLESSES HIS PEOPLE WITH PEACE.

—Psalm 29:11